The Active Ingredient is YOU

Published by Chris Edge ISBN 978-1-387-17848-3
Cover Design by Rob Whiteside

www.theactiveingredientisyou.com

for Jenny...

The Active Ingredient is YOU

Chris Edge

Ingredients

Ingredients

A Quick Note

For a period of three years, I was writing for AllAccess.com. It started out as a column about digital technology, but it quickly turned into a column about leadership, brand building, and engaging audiences.

When I started writing, I often saw things through the lenses of my kids, at the time seven and nine years old. I was drawn to their perspectives and experiences. They had a unique way of looking at the world.

Emily and Max, now both in high school, never had a chance to read these stories. I'm hoping now they do and that this book will provide some inspiration.

At the very least, I want them to understand one very simple principle...making things better, achieving goals, getting things done, actually starts with them.

They are the Active Ingredient in their lives, just like you are in yours.

The
Active
Ingredient
is YOU

The Active Ingredient...is You

Read the label on any drug, and it will tell you what the Active Ingredient is...the substance that's biologically active. There's other stuff in there, but the compound that will make a difference, that can affect change, that can make things better, is the active ingredient (AI).

If I read the drug facts on the side of your box, the box referring to your work (and your life), what would it say? Who or what would be listed as the active ingredient?

In order for your team to create and deliver, there needs to be guidance. There needs to be someone calling the shots and empowering others to be the best that they can be.

I think it's you.

A Penis Can Teach You About Branding

My son walked into the kitchen, he was wearing jeans. He's seven, thinks he's cool, and probably is.

"Hey Dad"

"Yeah buddy?"

"You see this?"

At this moment I look at my son...he is pointing to the zipper fly on his jeans.

"That's me...my penis."

My son had just pointed out he had a boner and was rather proud of it.

Sometimes, even though we think people know what we are or what we do, they don't. Even though it's clear to us what our brands are about, it's not for others. I looked at what my son was pointing at and still didn't get it until he told me.

Assuming what you have created is worthy of consumption, ask yourself:

- Do they know what we are?
- How will they use us?
- Are we worth talking about?
- How are we communicating our benefits?

They don't always see what you see. Sometimes you have to point it out.

Willy Wonka Makes Your Brand Better!

When I worked in Indianapolis, there was a chocolate shop on the first floor of our building that sold hot apple cider. It was awesome...my morning guy and I would jump down there a couple of times a week during the winter (which in Indy is about ten months long).

The Chocolate Company had cases and cases of chocolate, ice cream, and a giant copper kettle that dispensed liquids, mainly my cider. It looked like something right out of Willy Wonka.

One day I ordered the cider, and rather than watch this magical stuff come out of the copper kettle, I heard this from the employee.

"Where's the Apple Juice? We ran out."

Where's the Apple Juice? Are you f***ing kidding me? Here I thought the Oompa Loompas were out back stirring freshly smashed apples into a giant bowl with cinnamon, and really it's just some kid with a plastic bottle of apple juice that I can buy for a buck and half at the grocery store.

I never bought it again.

The power of the experience, the story
they told, had worked. I was buying
two dollar cups of cider every week.

They Wonkafied it!

What about you? When people use
your stuff, your ideas, your website,
your widgets, what kind of experience
are they having? What would Willy
Wonka do to your brand?

Stories sell. Start telling one.

You Should Quit...I Did

I'm done, tired, calling it in. I'm out of gas, indifferent, closed. Not interested in what's next, or how to get there. I'm tired of fighting, debating, and certainly sick of listening. I don't care, I'm not interested, and if I was, I certainly wouldn't admit it. I've already told you, I quit.

You may not know this, but this is my first time. Quitting that is. I don't make it a habit to give up, walk away, and leave people hanging. I'm just doing it this one time. I don't know what you'll do, I don't really care, I don't think you do either which is why I'm quitting.

Except I'm not really quitting, I'm just saying that out loud, because it's liberating. It makes me feel better, it makes me feel like I have a choice (because I do...I just sometimes forget that). I took a stand, put my foot down, and told myself this is the end.

Except it's not, I've decided I'm going to work harder, smarter, faster, and better than anybody you could possibly replace me with. It turns out, after being unemployed for thirty seconds, I'm ready to come back and kick some ass...including yours.

I'm energized, alive, fueled up, and ready to go. I figured out what's next, and I'm headed there right now. Are you coming?

Belief

I've been watching a series called "When We Left Earth: The NASA Missions". It's the remarkable story of how NASA landed a man on the moon in less than ten years. It's the story of how smart engineers, pilots, and scientists had the audacity to put human beings on top of a thirty five story rocket that held a million gallons of fuel, and shoot them into space.

It's insanity in action.

Three astronauts died while training for Apollo 1, Neil Armstrong himself was ejected horizontally out of a craft while training, shit broke, didn't fit, exploded, and caught fire.

They never stopped.

Why?

Belief is why things are created, why we innovate, why we accomplish things that we aren't sure we can.

Belief is powerful.

Forward progress stops when you stop believing in where you're going and what you're doing.

Believing in the unbelievable is what makes things possible.

They put a man on the moon. What will you accomplish?

What Character Traits Would You Choose?

If before you were born you could select five character traits to define you and take with you for the rest of your life; what would they be? Would you choose to be happy, humble, or hopeful? How about the internal drive to succeed, patience, or perhaps intuitiveness?

My ten year old son thought of four:

- Happy
- Funny
- Creative
- Nice

I pressed, wondering if these were traits he wanted or if in fact he thought he already had. It was the latter, he really just described himself.

Did you do the same? Did you simply define who you think you are or the person you'd like to be? For a long time now I have had two items on my list. Two things that I think above all others make things like happiness, compassion, or humility easier to come by.

1.   **Adaptability**

How well do you handle change in the office or at home? Everything is constantly changing; the more flexible you are the more you'll enjoy the ride.

2.   Patience

As much as I believe that making gut
decisions, tracking down a hunch and
taking risks are essential to advancing
our teams and projects, the approach
is better if you pause for second to
consider all your options. You'll need
this while your ideas incubate and
develop.

So how about you, what's that list
look like?

A 7 Year Old Simplifies my Brand

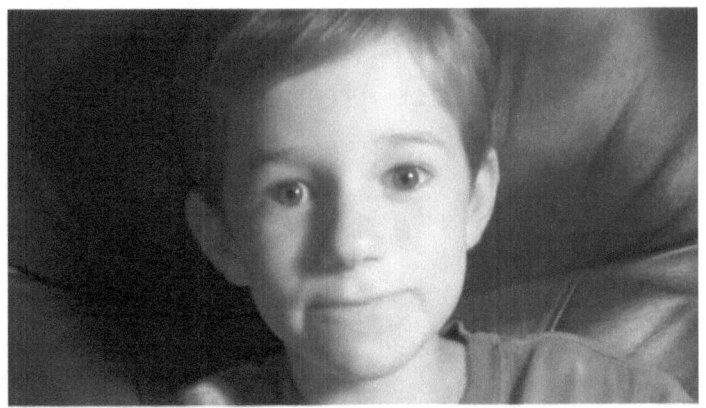

"He gets paid to ride bikes?"

"Yes" I said. "It takes a lot of work to be that good, but yes Lance gets paid to ride his bike."

"Seriously...that would be so cool."

This conversation took place with my son last weekend. We went for a bike ride and somebody passing us yelled to him, "Come on Lance, you can do it". Max had no clue that the Lance reference was about Austin resident and cyclist Lance Armstrong.

How amazing that a man who won the Tour De France a record seven times had his career reduced to six words by a seven year old; "he gets paid to ride bikes".

Not old enough to know too much and not young enough to know too little. At seven your world is clean and simple. Things are black and white, either this or that, there is no in between.

I wonder if what you think you are or what you want to be is really how people perceive you. If you asked Lance Armstrong what his brand is, I think his response might be more than, "I get paid to ride bikes".

I also wondered what Max would say about my radio station. He listens to it quite a bit. I'm sure it started because Dad worked there, but I can honestly tell you he digs the station. I wonder what Max thinks KGSR is. I wonder what he would say it does.

I decided to ask. He had no idea this was coming. Here's his unedited, unfiltered, unprepared response.

"Plays music...plays commercials..."

He paused, looked up and put his finger on his chin. Then the light bulb went off and he looked at me.

"...helps charity?"

Indeed.

Like he did for Lance, Max summed up what KGSR does in six words. I would suggest finding a seven year old kid who likes what you do. You might learn something about your brand.

My Kid Peed in the Backyard

I asked my eight year old son to take the dog out to relieve herself. The dog, and the responsibility, is fairly new, so I intended to go with him. He had a head start, because I fumbled around for shoes. Eventually, I strolled across the back of my house and turned left to head down the side. There it was... a glorious stream, not from the dog, but from my son.

That's right; my son was peeing with the dog. She's squatting, and he's standing with one hand on the leash and the other...well you get the idea.

Just because the dog does it, doesn't mean you get to do it. Lesson #86 of a gazillion he's heard from me over the years like:

Because...
- we take turns
- your teeth will fall out
- we have a penis
- you can't fit under the bed
- the bed won't make itself
- you'll get sick if you eat it
- you have a fever
- if you don't pick it up I keep it
- you can't
- I said so

My radio station is not #1, I'm not out of debt, we don't live near family, and when the toilet flushes on the second floor above my office at work, I can hear it. Life isn't fair.

Say these words with me: "It is what it is".

Now get on with doing what you do, as well as you can do it.

OPEN or CLOSED?

I have something to say, and I hope you're OPEN to it.

Without limitless curiosity, we in fact, become limited.

This is one of the many things that makes being a human being so fricking cool. We are constantly curious about all sorts of things. Unfortunately, sometimes we become selective about what we want to hear.

Being OPEN is fatiguing. There's a lot of stuff coming at you, and it's not always easy to keep up and process all those ideas and suggestions. If you were a retailer, a mom and pop grocery store for example, what sign would be hanging in the front window?

Are you OPEN or CLOSED?

If you're CLOSED, it's over. You don't care anymore. You have all the answers and there's really nothing worth opening the door for.

You're tired of listening.

If you're OPEN, you're ready. You're curious about how things look and feel through the lenses of others. Capable and willing to try, fail, or better yet, succeed.

It's easier to be CLOSED. Focused on yourself, your belief systems, knowing you're right...even when you may not be. Being OPEN is much harder. Its admitting every day that you don't have all the answers (Hint: We already know you don't).

Collaborating on projects and getting different perspectives can help you chase down hunches, find solutions, and create what's next for you, your business, or the things worth working on.

Yes!

You played hard...did you work hard?

When you were asked to help out and cover someone else's job, did you say yes or make an excuse why you couldn't?

When they asked if you were interested in learning how, did you let the fear of not being good at it stop you or drive you?

When you fell into that "opportunity", did you embrace it or pass the work on to someone else?

When you found yourself lost in a conversation, did you ask questions,

or nod your head in agreement and
fake understanding?

When you said "no", you really
couldn't, or you were lazy?

Try answering like this and see what
happens:

- Yes
- I'll try it
- I can do this
- Teach me
- I will

In life, the more you can do for
yourself, the better off you'll be. The
same is true in the office.

The first step is saying yes.

What Kind of Action Figure are You?

For Father's day my kids got me an action figure of Albert Einstein. He's cool. I like him. Guess what he comes with, a piece of chalk. That's it, one of the greatest thinkers in the history of the world, the father of modern physics and owner of arguably the most recognizable equation in the universe ($E=MC^2$) comes with a lousy piece of chalk.

Why? Because in the end, what Albert did was teach. He was a professor.

So why are you in business? Can you drill it down into a six inch piece of plastic? When customers walk down the toy aisle, will you have to create something that screams "pick me" in order to get noticed, or is your brand worth looking for?

Stop. Look. Listen.

I made a grocery run last weekend in pursuit of corn on the cob. Our grocer stages trash barrels so you can do the shucking on-site. I generally hate this job, but I had help, so my son and I got to work on four ears. After his first one, he looks up at me and says this:

"Can we do more than four? This is cool."

"Really?" I thought. "You want to just stand here and shuck corn?"

"Totally!"

We kept going, three then two more, then another three. We started handing them to strangers. We laughed, made fun of ourselves, and he kept telling me how great it was.

In the meantime, there was a guy running around in the tomatoes chatting with someone through his Bluetooth ear piece. He looked like an idiot. Two little ones in tow, he just wanted to get in, get out, and get some work done. He missed an opportunity to engage with his kids.

Connecting with your audience is no different. Sometimes we get so wrapped up in the transaction, that we miss out on listening and learning from them. That's the good stuff, that's where the great ideas and inspiration come from.

It's just like crossing the street:

Stop. Look. Listen.

If you don't do that, you'll never make it to the other side. If you don't do that with your customers, you won't get your brand to the next level either.

Things You Should Say at Work

This is a list of thoughts that I hope you and your teams are saying out loud inside your office or workspace. If not, copy or print this and keep it as a handy reminder.

It's far better for you to be thinking this way, rather than your competition.

Let's try it.
I have an idea!
What if I'm right?
What if we did this?
Have you tried this?
Ignore the research?
Let's go ask the intern.
What if it doesn't work?

Wait I'm on to something!

What if this actually works?

How would (others) manage this?

But that hasn't been done before?

I have a hunch, let's hash this out!

What would another department do?

Ask the receptionist what they think.

What if we listened to our customers?

What if we fail and are embarrassed?

How else can we use the technology?

I'm over thinking it, let's just do it.

Nobody else is doing it, why us?

A unique idea or rehash of old?

I'm not afraid, are you?

I don't know.

Yes we can!

It's Good Enough

It really is. The work you do is
meaningful. The work you do is
important to the success of your
company. It has impact...your
actions, your efforts, and your ideas.
It's not a fluke. You get "it" and you
know it. You should be proud of
yourself and recognize the difference
you make.

Don't get cocky though. You're not
<u>that</u> good.   You're good enough.
Learn humility, if you have to look it
up, do it. It's worth the read.

A lot of people respect you. Several
people in fact actually look up to you.
Really they do. They're people that you

wouldn't expect. There is even somebody out there who frequently tells the story about how you made a difference in their career. There's even one person whose life was changed because you listened. You made a difference.

I know you don't get the credit you think you deserve, I know it's tough when somebody else appears to be taking responsibility for the work that you did or the idea that you had, but that's life. It's not always fair.

The truth is, the people that need to know...know.

Flag Football Fail

I volunteered to help coach my son's flag football team. I'm the Defensive Coordinator. I have no idea what I'm doing, and it shows.

Two games deep into the season, and we can't stop a parked car.

Here's the problem. Nobody on the team has any idea what their specific job is. I'm trying to give every kid a chance to play each position, and what's happening is that nobody really understands fully how to play any of them.

Our teams at work face the same challenge; we have to provide clear lanes and clear direction or nobody will be able to drive down the field or make a play.

Do something crazy, sit down with each employee and ask them three questions.

"What do you think your job is?"

"Are you clear on what it is you need to do and how you can achieve your goals?"

"Is there anything I (the company) can do to support that effort?"

If things are working, this should be embarrassing, and you'll have a good laugh.

If things aren't, you'll figure out what needs to be fixed and fix it.

Start Strong, Finish Stronger

I spent my summers working for my uncle's construction company. On my first day on the job, I felt I had something to prove. I knew I'd get pegged as the "nephew". I didn't want to be labeled as the kid collecting a check without doing any real work. Here because he's family, not because he's any good at what he does.

The job site was on the campus of Mount Holyoke College. We were renovating an old dormitory, and it required removing the basement floor with jack hammers. They told me to grab a "J" Bar (think big giant iron bar about four feet tall) and start knocking out the concrete underneath the walls that divided the bedrooms.

I went nuts, worked nonstop for two hours. I was hunched over smashing the concrete, prying it out from under the wall, loading it into wheelbarrows and hauling it out. I was exhausted, I cut myself, I was filthy, and I was about to die.

The morning break rolled around, and I hit the grass outside and thought I was going to throw up. I almost did. This guy looks at me and says:

"What the f**k are you doing? You gotta pace yourself."

I had given everything I had to let the crew know that I was serious and here to work only to render myself useless the rest of the day.

Our careers are like this, relationships too, a lot of things are. We go all out at the start and as time goes by, we start running out of gas. The start is actually the easy part.

Sure you're nervous and unsure, but you're also loaded with excitement, energy, passion and belief in yourself. When this stuff wears off, you start doubting. You know what to do and how to do it, but suddenly you're not sure you can.

I'd tell you to be patient and start slow. But you won't. I'd tell you to pace yourself so you're consistent throughout, but you won't.

So go ahead... tear it up, blaze a path, lead the others, and when you run out of gas, understand that it's not the end. It's merely the middle, and the beginning of what's next.

Do What You Love

Michael J. Fox was on Regis & Kelly last week, and he told his story of becoming a professional actor. The Vancouver native was still in high school and asked his father if they could make the move to Hollywood so he could make a go at it. Michael asked with much trepidation and his father responded with this gem:

"If you want to be a lumber jack you got to go to the forest."

If you're a writer...write. If you're a singer...sing. If you're a leader, then start leading. If you're doing what you want to do, congratulations, most people aren't. If you're not doing what

you want...then get going. Surround
yourself with people who have skills or
qualities you admire...they'll rub off on
you...you'll get better, progress, and in
no time be cutting down trees in the
forest.

Maybe today's the day you pick up the
ax.

Brave Max

A month ago, while the two of us were goofing off with hockey sticks in the garage, my son announced to me that he wanted to play hockey. Skating only once in his life, he thought he'd be pretty good at it. I did some homework and found a free thirty minute introduction to skating class at the local rink and signed him up.

It was a month away; I thought Max might lose interest. He didn't. Instead, there was quite the buildup. It was like anticipating a vacation.

Questions from the eight year-old kept coming:

- What do I wear?
- Do we get to wear the pads?
- Can I be a goalie?
- Hockey gloves or regular gloves?
- Are there other kids?
- Who's teaching me?
- Can I play wing instead of goalie?
- I'm like in training right?

Last week, we drove to the rink, still excited; he put his sweatshirt, helmet and gloves on in the car before we left. We live in Texas, it was one hundred degrees, but he didn't care. He wanted to be a hockey player.

We checked in, I laced up the skates; he waited and continued to tell me how excited he was to get started. Everything was fine...until he stepped on the ice.

I was sitting behind the glass waiting to watch my smiling son take what we both thought would be his first strides into the world of hockey. He stumbled out there, lined up with two other kids, and then started to "skate".

Following the teachers instructions, he learned how to fall, turn, and push off. I could only see the back of his head. Tiny little guy out there next to a kid who was younger but a foot taller.

I watched Max drag his body to the blue line and then turn back to the boards. When he got there, he looked up at me. All I saw was fear. He was stunned. This wasn't easy. He didn't know what he was doing. He had already fallen three times. My heart sank.

For the next thirty minutes, I watched his little body get pummeled by the frozen ice. He fell on his ass, no joke... about fifteen times, then his knees, hands, and a couple of times on his hips. It was like watching your kid get beat up. Towards the end, he couldn't even stand on the skates.

He came off the ice and reached for my hand, we walked over to the bench, and I started unlacing his skates. He wouldn't look at me. His eyes went left, right, up, and down, it was all he could do to not make eye contact. I guess he felt like he had let me down, or he was embarrassed about not being any good. I asked how it went, and all I got was a muttered "good".

I don't know that I've ever felt that bad for someone. It was killing me. I thought I was going to cry, certainly choked up a little. Thirty minutes ago, he was confident, determined, ready, and above all...happy. Now he was crushed. It was awful.

We walked out to the car. I prepped my speech about how it was ok if he didn't want to go back. I thought about how important it was for him to know that I didn't care if he played hockey again, and that I was proud of him for trying.

We got to the car, I opened his door. He pulled his sore little legs into the back seat. Slid his sweatshirt off, and then turned his head to me and said this.

"Dad?"

"Yes Max?"

"Even though I fell down a lot, I think I'm gonna try again."

That's when I lost it. I honestly cried the entire ride home. That's my brave son back there.

Max teaches us that we must get up, we have to try. It doesn't matter if we make it or not, it's the process of trying that makes us better.

The Utility Player

You know who I'm talking about. This is the employee who seems to be good at a lot of different things. While we are focused on the big picture stuff, the little things are being taken care of by a team member we are not yet fully invested in.

They work their ass of while waiting for their chance to step up and make full-time contributions. They say yes to everything, work hard, and are seemingly available to play the role of an all-purpose employee whenever the need arises. For them, it's not about the money it's the experience, the networking, and the learning.

That is until it becomes about the money.

If you can move them into a full-time gig...you're lucky. That's the best case scenario. You've spent years developing this employee, they know your business, and they carry that passion for "doing" into their full-time gig.

Worst case scenario for you, not the employee, is that you lose them to another company. It's certainly great to see people you work with succeed, but it would be a lot better if they succeeded with you.

Take fifteen minutes right now to identify these people on your team.

Get a sense for where they want to go. One of the challenges for the utility player is that they tend to not have one thing they want to do...they're sort of all over the place in terms of career goals. If you help them focus, it may help focus you on finding a path they can take that keeps them in the building.

They are likely happy and engaged right now but soon they'll be ready for what's next. Will you be? Can you afford to lose them?

Are We Clear?

I was having breakfast last week with the family, and the topic of conversation turned to Osama Bin Laden. My wife and I thought we'd prep the kids for what could be discussed at school that day regarding the events of 9/11. Max thought he knew what went down:

"You ever hear of those Clear Bombs?"

"Clear Bombs?" I asked.

"Yeah dad, they're new."

For a moment, I really had no idea what he was talking about. He went on to tell me how his friend told him about these new "Clear Bombs" and how bad they were and if we wanted to get rid of bad guys, this was the way to go. He was pretty sure that's what must have happened in Pakistan.

"Max", I said, "Do you mean Nuclear Bombs?"

"Yeah dad, the new Clear Bombs."

A pretty heavy conversation continued about the events of 9/11 and the eventual capture of Osama Bin Laden, but I was also left with a far more frivolous thought about how we communicate with one another.

Max is a kid, I get it, but it got me thinking about that old game called

"Telephone". You whisper something into one person's ear, they pass it on to the next, and by the time you get to the last person, the message has changed.

If you're in charge of your brand's messaging, how many people does it have to pass through before it hits your target? Have you eliminated the potential for people to misunderstand what you're trying to communicate?

The message starts with you, then it's your employees, then it's the sneezers (folks who evangelize who you are), and so on. There are more links in the chain than you realize.

Two things you should do right now:

1. Make sure EVERYBODY on your team is clear on what and who you are.

2. Start engaging directly with the customer, 1:1, it's never been easier.

I'd hate for customers to decide they don't need or like you because of something you're not.

The Dog

I am not a cat person, or a dog person.
I suppose I'm a "kid person". I have
two. That is until now. This weekend,
we adopted a dog. She's two, calm,
sweet, and for the most part,
compliant; but make no mistake, our
hands are full. It's been less than a
week and, I've learned a couple of
things already.

- We can't make her do things she
  doesn't want to do herself. We'll

need to make an effort to show
what we expect, and she'll do the
same I suppose. It's going to
take hours and a lot of
consistent effort.

- She's still not convinced we
  mean well. She wants to believe
  that things are going to work out,
  but she's pensive, always
  watching to see if we are as
  genuine as we claim to be.

- There are basic needs that have
  to be met. If we fail on these, it's
  over.

- She's clearly a financial
  investment. Taking care of her
  will cost money. Most expensive

thus far are the things that make her feel like our home is her home.

Perhaps the "she" in this story could easily be the "she" that listens to your radio station, shops your store, or buys your product. We think it's good enough to unlock the door, turn on the music, or make the widget. It's usually not.

Got a dog? Pet? How about a kid? Look at them, how did you build that relationship, how long did it take? Was it worth it to get to where you are now?

That's what I thought.

Success is a Team Sport

What good is success if you're not able to share it? You created something memorable but alienated your staff and co-workers on the way to the finish line. You stand there in all your glory...alone. It works this way in your personal life too, success matters but how you get there matters too.

Human beings crave relationships. We love sharing ourselves with others, we like when people share themselves with us. This is why social media works, why it's fun to watch sports, and why faith matters so much to our species. Finding commonalities among us bring us closer together.

Don't be the guy that walks around the office yelling "we did it" when in fact nobody feels like they did.

Empower those around you to be difference makers. The journey and the end results are more meaningful when you have others you can share the success with.

If the Pope Can do it, You Can Too!

The Holy Father has received the
kind letter sent to him and he has asked
the Secretariat of State to express his
thanks and to convey his blessing.

Monsignor G.B. Re
Assessor

When I was nine years old, I wrote a
letter to then President Jimmy Carter
and asked him to save the whales. He
sent a glossy magazine about the
White House and how cool he was.
Meh. Later that same year, I tried
hittin' up the Pope. The Vatican
responded with a typed letter, on
official letterhead, and signed it by
hand.

I'm still impressed.

All we have to do now is type and then click "send". Seems effortless doesn't it?

Taking the time to send a meaningful response allows you to make a remarkable impact on the person who took the time to reach out to you.

I think it's worth doing. You?

Do Your Customers Understand You?

Try reading this.

Ddi yuo kwno taht teh hmuna biarn cna rade txet enve if teh ltetsre rae in hte worgn pcela? Taht's becesue hte barin rades teh etrnie wrod, nto jstu het dinidivula ltetres.

Pretty cool right?

If you couldn't read it, here's what it said.

Did you know that the human brain can read text even if the letters are in the wrong place? That's because the brain reads the entire word, not just the individual letters.

I was driving back from the grocery
store this week and in front of me was
a cyclist trying to tell me which way
they were going to turn. I say trying,
because prior to turning right, they
stuck their left arm out and bent the
forearm up at the elbow. If I was a
cyclist or understood the signals then
I would have been prepared for the
right turn. I would have understood
sticking out your left arm, with your
forearm up, means they're turning
right.

My wife would have killed this person.
Most people would expect you to point
to the right to indicate turning right. I
only understood the signals because
of all the times I followed my dad in

his old British car (MG) with its faulty blinkers.

It got me thinking about how our brands communicate. The terminology that we use makes sense in our circles and in the business that we are in but not always to the end user.

Our brains might be able to read words that are spelled wrong, but it takes some focus on the reader's part. I'll bet your brand isn't so powerful that your customers stop what they're doing to try to figure out what you're saying.

Communicate with words and in ways that everybody understands. If not you're missing out on potential customers, listeners, audiences, consumers, or fans. I'll let you pick the right adjective.

STOP YELLING!

Last week, I attended another one of my daughter's swim meets. This time around, something struck me, or rather interrupted me. It was Moms and Dads screaming words of "encouragement" from the side of the pool.

Hey parents....guess what?

THEY CAN'T HEAR YOU!

They're listening to their coaches, the kid next to them who farted, and oh by the way...

THEY'RE DIVING INTO A POOL AND GOING UNDERWATER!

They are swimming, focused, and determined...thinking about the impending flip turn, or if their arms are in the right position. I know you mean well, but rather than encouraging your kid, you're making the rest of us crazy. I won't even get into how ridiculous you look cheering for a kid who is UNDERWATER!

Why do I mention this? It's not because I think these parents are crazy, it's because they are exactly like old school marketers. Yelling about how great their products are through billboards, TV, radio, and worst of all...print.

Nobody is listening...they're busy.

Perhaps parents should be letting the coaches coach; the swimmers swim, and try encouraging kids in those moments when they give you their attention.

Are you doing the same with your brand? Are you yelling or engaging? There's a difference.

Evelyn Said "Hi"

Last week, I was getting the oil changed in my car. It's early, nobody wants to talk, but there we are; four adults with our heads in our screens. Aside from a glance or two, content with minding our own business.

On my left, I see a tiny person, a four to five year old little girl who I think has something to say. She's standing a few feet from me, staring, waiting for something. I notice she takes another deliberate step and stops. When I make eye contact with her, she raises her hand and simply says... "Hi".

We start chatting, she asks if I like coffee, then she tells me about her

favorites...milk, water, and juice
adding that, "It's important to stay
hydrated". I ask what her name is,
and she not only offers it up but spells
it for me.

"E-V-E-L-Y-N."

The lobby of the dealership lights up,
her dad has something to say, the
woman across from me spending close
to a grand on her radiator isn't
bothered by that much anymore.

Evelyn did something most adults just
don't do anymore. She said hi.
Maybe what we all really need to be
doing is taking a minute to put down
the technology and talk to each other.

Let's make it a point to have real relationships with our audiences, in person! You don't have to have anything to say. Things will come up; you just have to say hi.

Let's Kill Animals for Fun!

We can put live animals on a Great Lakes Schooner, set it on fire, and then sail the damn thing right over Niagara Falls. We can use bears, buffalo, foxes, dogs, cats and whatever else we can find in the woods. They'll be on fire, running around on the deck! We'll invite people to watch. Everyone will be talking about it. It's gonna be great!

Crazy?

Yes it is, but, in fact, it happened. In the early 1800's, business owners did this to drum up tourism in and around Niagara Falls. Over 20,000 people came to watch this "event".

With all the effort we put into trying to get noticed in the attention economy, how close do you get to the line of impropriety. How outrageous is too outrageous? Is the attention worth alienating fans? Maybe for a change, we should go the other way and get noticed for something meaningful.

For a while now, there's been a trend in syncing community outreach efforts with business. Buy a car and we'll give your charity 500 bucks. Buy this yogurt, and we'll donate 10% to breast cancer research. Every time you buy a kids meal, a penny goes to this non-profit.

What about your brand, are you involved in Cause Marketing? When's the last time you got recognition for making a significant impact in your community? How often do you do it?

I'll argue that this attention lasts longer, runs deeper, and is a lot more meaningful to your audience.

Screaming how outrageous you are doesn't seem to work anymore.

Could you Stop the Bleeding?

A while back, I was buying a Blu-Ray player at a big box store. I was in the process of checking out when a frantic mom with a kid about four years old came running up to the register in Electronics. There I was with the cashier, the mom...and her bleeding four year old son. That's right, he was bleeding. I don't mean fell down cut your knee bleeding...I mean fell face first into a metal shelf and ripped open your chin, lips, and nose bleeding.

It was bad.

Mom was in panic mode and had simply run to the nearest employee and asked for help. Too bad it was my man No-Action Jackson. This guy just froze. She's screaming for help and he picks up a phone and calls somebody else while the kid kept bleeding.

When he doesn't get an answer from the manager, he tries calling another manager. Of course, the kid keeps bleeding.

All of it unfolding before my eyes, he's on the phone, she's freaking out, and the kid's screaming. I realized that what she really needed was a way to stop the bleeding, like maybe the paper towels sitting on the counter.

I grabbed them and handed to mom...you would have thought I gave that woman a hundred bucks.

Old man winter was still on the phone.

How come that guy had no idea what to do? How come rather than dealing with the situation himself he avoided it? Why was it not obvious to him that the paper towels would make some immediate sense until someone arrived?

Perhaps it's just that I had the benefit of being a spectator, it was easy to remain calm and assess. He was expected to solve the problem and solve it immediately. I'm guessing this retailer doesn't have a section in the training manual called, "What to do when a kid starts bleeding buckets at your register".

When things go wrong at work, what do you do? I don't mean a bleeding kid, I mean when revenue is down? When there's a typo in the six figure marketing campaign, when a customer is pissed about an experience, when you or someone on your staff has royally f'd up and you're left holding the bag?

What you do matters. That reaction is the key difference between those who can lead organizations and those who can't. Know how to solve problems, it's one of the best skills you can have.

We are Defined by Moments

We are defined by moments. We all have them. Fleeting, yes, but they happen. Good ones inspire us, bad ones hurt...both define who we are.

There's a book festival here in Austin every year, and last fall my nine year old daughter and I decided to attend. She's an avid reader, writes short stories and poems, and one of her favorite authors was speaking.

We crammed into a small church, sat about three rows back, and waited for Meg Cabot to take the stage. What I thought I was waiting for was an author to tell her story of pain and suffering, the rejection and the celebration of chasing a book deal. I got that.

What I didn't expect was how big of a moment this was going to be for my daughter. I realized I had a front row seat for her experience...her moment. Meg started speaking, and I thought to myself...

"Please don't let her down."

Emily sat on the edge of her seat, listening with not just her ears, but her whole being. Meg indeed spoke of writing story after story and getting rejected every time; struggling with criticism, and then reaching a level of success she had not expected.

I put my arm around my daughter. She looked up at me, smiled, and whispered…"Thanks Dad."

This is what life is about. Creating an atmosphere for you and for others to experience things that motivate and inspire us to be better people than we think we are capable of being.

Be Aware. Be Open. Be Ready.

This is your moment.

Salt & Pepper, Time & Temp

There's an awarding winning barbecue
joint here in Austin. It started out as a
trailer and soon graduated into its
own building. The barbecue is so
good that you have to line up at 10:30
in the morning, wait an hour until
they open the doors at 11:30, and
when the meat is gone...they close.
I'm not kidding.

This past summer, Bon Appétit
magazine called it the Best Barbecue
in America.

Aaron Franklin was asked by our local
news what his secret was; I'm
paraphrasing but this was his
response:

We get the best meat from Montana, and then it's about salt and pepper, time and temp. That's it.

Really? No secret sauce? He's not blending 200 spices together, or using his great granddaddy's recipe?

How many times have we messed something up, failed at making something better, because we kept piling on all of our little tricks.

How many times have we rushed to decisions, because we didn't have the patience to just let it be, and see it through?

The recipe for success here can easily be translated to your life and your work. Don't over season, make sure the basics are being executed, and above all...be patient.

Encouragement in Disguise

On a flight from Raleigh to Hartford, I sat with my ten year old son and listened to him ramble on for almost 90 minutes. It was beautiful, at times incoherent, but beautiful.

Two rows up from us in an aisle seat was a little old lady. She looked lived in, hunched over - her hair dyed red, frail but stable, wearing a Yankees ball cap and chewing a piece of gum. Midway through the flight, she turned to both of us and then looked my son straight in the eye. With her right index finger gently tapping the side of her head, she said this:

"Your father's a smart man."

And with that, she abruptly turned back around.

I was puzzled. Why did that happen? Why did she do that? Did she really think I was smart? Do I look smart? Is it the glasses? Could she hear what Max and I were talking about earlier? Had I said something smart? That's a lot of pressure to put on me! Now my son thinks I'm smart. What if I'm not? Hey lady, knock that shit off, it's hard enough being a parent without the expectation from your kids that you might actually know what you're doing.

Perhaps it isn't what she said, but what we heard. I've believed for a long time that people come in and out of our lives with purpose. You do the same to others. I've written a few things on this and simply put I think I needed that. Encouragement comes in clever doses sometimes. The real shame in these moments of impact would be not listening and not receiving the note.

Was this a message for Max to remind him that his father, misguided at times, won't lead him astray?

Was it a message for Dad to remind him that maybe he's capable of more than he thinks?

Something tells me she knew exactly what she was doing.

Believing it Through

How many times have you said this?

"That's a great idea...I should do that."

Except you don't.

Seeing it through is not the same as believing it through. Imagining how you get something done and what the end result looks like is different from believing what the end looks like.

You have to believe the results are going to be there, so it can motivate you to plow through all the crap it's going to take to get there.

Culture is Defined by What You Tolerate

You don't like it? I blame you. That's right, it's your fault.

Culture is defined by what you tolerate.

- Bad employees
- Mediocre performance
- Lack of innovation

These issues exist because you allow them to. It applies in the home as well.

- Kids back talking
- Messy room
- General disrespect
- Tension with spouse

Instead of blaming everybody else, or external influences, you have to consider the role that you play.

The culture in your home or office, the atmosphere that exists...doesn't just exist. It's fostered and managed by you. You allow for things to happen or not.

Define your culture and drive it...if not, the negative culture will drive you.

Do "It" Now

I have a cool aunt. She lived well, made smart decisions, served her country, had a strong faith, retired early in '06 and moved to her dream home on the lake.

Then she died.

Bummer...finally got to a place in her life where she could slow down and enjoy it, and God had other plans.

Whatever it is you want to do, do "it" now. Now is a good time.

Build it, create it, share it, or sell it. Buy it, drive it, visit it, or welcome it. Quit it, grab it, love it or leave it. It's time.

We're all supposed to plan for the future, be patient and let things evolve or come to us. Work hard to achieve things and then enjoy. I get it. But you don't get to decide how much time you have.

Get busy.

Lessons Learned in the Hiring Process

Here are four things I learned while interviewing people for a position with my radio station.

- In an era of transparency and authenticity, it's hard to sell yourself. There's a fine line between bragging and sharing.

- Most people don't really believe they are good enough when in fact...they are. This is unfortunate.

- The perception we have of ourselves is often fueled by the circle of friends, family, and co-workers in orbit around us.

When you step outside the circle, you experience what others think of you for the very first time. It can be humbling.

- The more qualified your candidates are, the harder it is to determine who is the best person for the job. To resolve this, you have to make unscientific, intuitive based decisions.

One final thought for anybody applying for a job - it's not personal. Just because one person doesn't see greatness in your resume or see the spark inside you doesn't mean you don't have it. It just means this person didn't see it or was looking for something else.

Take the criticism, good and bad, and apply it. Be thankful you didn't get a job with a manager that didn't get you.

That wouldn't have been much fun.

BOOM!

You hear that? Feel that? See that?

Someone made an impact... was it
you?

Did you shock the world?

Did you close the deal, hit the mark,
hire the star, fire the dud, share your
faith, win the game, get the ratings, or
make the money?

Did you reach, achieve, accomplish,
attain? Complete, conquer, do, or
make?

Have you arrived?

Are you the one that went the extra mile, yard, meter, foot, or inch?

Was it you that said, "I can" when everybody else said, "I can't"?

Did you say "Yes" when the rest said "No"?

BOOM!

Was that you? I thought so.

Go get'm player.

What Matters

My daughter is nine. She likes to swim. This summer, we signed her up for swim league. It's legit, they practice daily, and on Saturdays, there's an eight hour swim meet. No joke, it's eight hours, and your kid only swims like three to five times for about a minute each. They keep meticulous track of how fast they are. There are three timers in each lane and then the average time sticks. Your kid's score gets collected and brought to the proofing table, and then it's checked for errors and signed off on before it's entered into the computer.

So after several meets with my daughter's times getting slower and slower she finally had "the week". She bested her times in three different strokes and in one case was almost six seconds faster. She was beaming.

I wanted to tell her how proud I was of her for swimming faster and before it came out of my mouth, I stopped.

Why?

I didn't want her to think it mattered. I didn't want her to think that swimming faster means something...that ranking 19th instead of 34th was important. It's not. What matters is that she tried her best, she never gave up, she didn't crash into her lane rope and that she had improved her dive. What matters is that she leaves practice smiling, that she makes new friends and that regardless of what her rank is, that she has fun being the best person she can be.

You see where I'm going with this don't you? This isn't just good advice for raising a strong confident kid; it's good advice for running your business.

Every month some measurement tool is going to tell you where you ranked.

Don't let it tell you if you're good at your job. Don't let it tell you if you're working hard enough, smart enough, or if you have what it takes to be the best brand you can be, because you already know you do. I know we can't ignore it, but you can put it in perspective.

You know what you're doing, just do it!

Impact Drives Action

Today there was a shooting on the campus of the University of Texas. Everything stopped. Everything. The second events like this happen our lives pause, the agenda gets derailed, and we stop working, stop thinking about the usual stuff, and start seeking. We want answers about who, what, when, where, and why. When a forty acre university campus gets put on lockdown, everybody pays attention, but what about all the other events in our lives?

What about the events that impact only us or a handful of people around us? Finding out you have cancer, a death in the family, the birth of a child?

Impact Drives Action

Instead of waiting to be impacted by a person, event, or a situation, why not do something now.

- Take the job
- Say you're sorry
- Go on vacation
- Quit (not the same as giving up)
- Say I love you
- Volunteer
- Call
- Offer to help
- Ask for forgiveness
- Forgive
- Finish

- Get started

- Do something

You could wait to be impacted in a way that motivates you to take action, or you can take action and be the one to make an impact.

I Still Don't Like the New York Yankees

Oh man. Maybe I do have an issue. Last week, my son was getting ready for school and walked out wearing a replica of a New York Yankees jersey. I must have stared at it for several minutes while this dialogue was running through my head.

"What the hell is that? Who gave him that? Why do I care? I don't even watch baseball anymore. People will think we like the Yankees. He's gonna get pounded by some kid with a wicked hook from Southey. Shit. I'm not going to say anything am I? He's his own person. He doesn't even get why this is wrong. It's just a game."

It's just a game. Why does this bother me? Although I'm a Massachusetts native, went to Yastrzemski's last game at Fenway, played catch with my friends while doing play by play using names like Rice, Evans, Lynn, Boggs, and the like, I haven't followed baseball for quite some time. Can't remember the last time I watched the Sox. Not sure what happened, but after they won the World Series for the first time, I sort of checked out.

So here's my kid in a Yankees jersey and suddenly baseball matters. In a second, I'm a proud member of Red Sox Nation and pissed.

Does your brand matter enough; does it evoke that kind of emotion when

your customers have stopped using
you? Probably not. Creating
passionate fans usually doesn't
happen overnight. What the Yankees
are is consistent. Since 1923, they've
won twenty seven world titles, forty
pennants, sixteen division titles and
three wild card berths. Love'm or
hate'm, that's a consistent history of
winning. How consistent is your
brand?

Execute. Execute. Execute. The
passion from the customer will follow.

The Rubber Brick

My middle school had an indoor swimming pool. Two reasons why this was bad...first off, it meant I had to see other naked guys. Not that there's anything wrong with that, it's just that in middle school you can't help but look and compare. It's the time in your life when everybody has varying degrees of body hair. We look ridiculous.

The second reason why this is abysmal was swim class. What a mess. The kids that could swim had the time of their life. They also had swim goggles. I was not as fortunate. I could swim alright if my eyes were closed, but I couldn't (wouldn't?) open them under water.

Now enter the "Rubber Brick". Seriously...this was a brick coated in thick rubber and used to torture young middle school kids like me. The teacher would throw the brick in the deep end of the pool while each student took turns diving after it.

I remember, I was clinging to the edge of the pool putting off this torture as long as I could. I had no idea how this was going to work. "If I can't open my eyes underwater, I can't see the brick. If I can't see the brick, I can't get it."

Kid after kid, dive after dive, one after another like missiles they dove down and came up with rubber gold. Each time, it was getting closer to my turn. I tried convincing my buddy, John (resident swim star), to loan me his goggles. John, being an ass, kept refusing.

Then, in slow motion (because it's my story and I can do that), the rubber brick was launched into the pool. The teacher blew the whistle and called my name.

"ccchhhrriiisssssssssssssssssssssssss!"

I remember thinking if I jump after it now, I can dive out with my arms extended, and it will just hit me.

I release my hand from the side of the pool, head toward the most embarrassing moment of my life, and as luck would have it, the bell rings. Shock! Relief! A wink! Was that a wink? Yes, it was...from the teacher.

She let me off, she knew.

We want all our stories to end with success and accomplishment, but sometimes they don't. Sometimes they just sink. The good news is those failures build your character...one brick at a time.

Fail

It's my new favorite four letter
word...fail. We spend a lot of time
trying not to, afraid of the result, the
ramifications, the embarrassment,
when in fact, failing might be what we
all need to do to get to what's next.

Here's what happens-somebody has a
great idea, they tell a colleague, maybe
they start trying to execute, at some
point they start applying science.

They start over thinking it, the idea
becomes complicated, watered down
or turns into something else entirely
and they give up.

How about this...maybe we stop over thinking it? What if, instead, we change our approach and rather than analyze, we simply try. Your ideas don't have to be finished or polished; that can happen while you're working it out.

You'll find great success in failing if you allow yourself to do it.

Perspective, Get Some!

I dare you to stand up on your desk. I'm being serious...stand on top of your desk, or the conference room table, or go surprise the receptionist. Take it a step further, go outside and stand up on top of your car, the roof of the building you're in, or a bench at the park across the street.

I dare you.

Why? Because this is what it will take for you to move forward. Your radio station, your digital strategies, your entire brand is depending on you to think differently and the only way to do that is to see differently. Getting above the day to day operations of your business will allow you to see things you can't when you're in the middle of today's latest crisis.

Have you ever gone on vacation, came back, and suddenly your brand (my radio station) didn't look/sound as good as you thought it did? Your surroundings and time away allowed you to return with a fresh set of eyes and ears. Maybe this should happen more than a few times a year?

Here's another idea. Take your entire staff on a field trip to Wal-Mart. This is your audience. They're not all pretty, or cool, stylish or trendy. They're not just the stereotypes you think are your customers. This is the "real" audience.

Getting perspective gets you to challenge what you do and believe to be truths about the way you program and deliver content on your frequency and digital platforms.

The Beginning

The book might be over, but what about you? Is this the beginning of what's next or the end?

You are the Active Ingredient!

Get Going!

 Father, Husband, Broadcaster and Personality Chris Edge can now add Author to the list. In his first book, "The Active Ingredient is You", Edge shares his thoughts on leadership, brand building, and connecting with audiences, most of which comes with perspective inspired by his young children.

Edge currently resides in Raleigh, North Carolina with his wife Jennifer, two teenagers, and an anxious dog named Daisy.